Vocabulary

This book belongs to

....

Colour the star when you complete a page.
See how far you've come!

☆4 ☆5 ☆6 ☆7 ☆8 ☆9 ☆10 ☆11
☆12 ☆13 ☆14 ☆15 ☆16 ☆17 ☆18 ☆19
☆20 ☆21 ☆22 ☆23 ☆24 ☆25 ☆26 ☆27
☆28 ☆29 ☆30 ☆31

Author: Becky Hempstock

How to use this book

- Your child will only need a writing pencil and some coloured crayons to be able to complete this book.

- Find a quiet, comfortable place to work, away from distractions.

- Help your child by reading the instructions and where necessary explain further what is needed to complete the task.

- At the top of each page is a table with new vocabulary which links to the topic and/or experience. Encourage your child to read each word and check their understanding.

- Encourage your child to complete the task using the new vocabulary. This will reinforce their understanding.

- If an activity is too difficult for your child, move on to another page and return to it at a later stage. The activities should be challenging but also achievable. Children need to feel they are successful to be inspired to continue.

- Always end each activity before your child gets tired so they will be eager to return the next time. Learning should be fun and rewarding, not a chore.

- Help and encourage your child to check their own answers as they complete each activity.

- To embed the new vocabulary, encourage your child to use each word in a full sentence.

- An even better way to embed new vocabulary is to experience it by going on a bus, visiting a hairdresser, taking a train journey, visiting a park and the beach. Have fun!

- Let your child return to their favourite pages once they have been completed.

- Talk about the activities they enjoyed and what they have learnt.

Special features of this book:

- **Familiar topics:** many topics should be relatable to things your child has seen or read about whilst possibly adding a few new words to extend their vocabulary.

- **Learning tip:** situated at the bottom of every left-hand page, this gives you some suggested talking points based around the page topic and experience. There is also an additional task should you wish to engage further with your child.

ACKNOWLEDGEMENTS
Published by Collins
An imprint of HarperCollins*Publishers* Ltd
The News Building
1 London Bridge Street
London
SE1 9GF

HarperCollins*Publishers*
1st Floor, Watermarque Building, Ringsend Road,
Dublin 4, Ireland

First published 2022
© HarperCollins*Publishers* Limited 2022

10 9 8 7 6 5 4 3 2

ISBN 978-0-00-849176-5

All images and illustrations are
© Shutterstock.com and
© HarperCollins*Publishers* Ltd

The author asserts the moral right to be identified as the author of this work.

All rights reserved. No part of this publication may be reproduced, stored in a retrieval system, or transmitted, in any form or by any means, electronic, mechanical, photocopying, recording or otherwise, without the prior permission of Collins.

British Library Cataloguing in Publication Data.

A Catalogue record for this publication is available from the British Library.

Author: Becky Hempstock
Publisher: Fiona McGlade
Editor and project manager: Chantal Addy
Cover Design: Sarah Duxbury and Amparo Barrera
Text Design and Layout: Sarah Duxbury, Ian Wrigley and Contentra Technologies Ltd
Production: Karen Nulty
Printed in India by Multivista Global Pvt. Ltd.

MIX
Paper from responsible source
FSC C007454

This book is produced from independently certified FSC™ paper to ensure responsible forest management.

For more information visit:
www.harpercollins.co.uk/green

Contents

How to use this book — 2
The toy shop — 4
Visiting the vets — 5
Going on a bus — 6
Park life — 7
At the supermarket — 8
The seaside — 9
I can see a rainbow — 10
A football match — 11
A day on a building site — 12
The doctors' surgery — 13
Houses and homes — 14
At school — 15
Into space — 16
Can you fix it? — 17
Nocturnal creatures — 18
Fruit smoothie fun — 19
At the farm — 20
Eating out — 21
A new baby — 22
Sports — 23
Weather — 24
Hairdressers / Barbers — 25
Famous cities and landmarks — 26
Emergency services — 27
Recycling — 28
Flying high — 29
Train journey — 30
KS1 common exception words — 31
Answers — 32

The toy shop

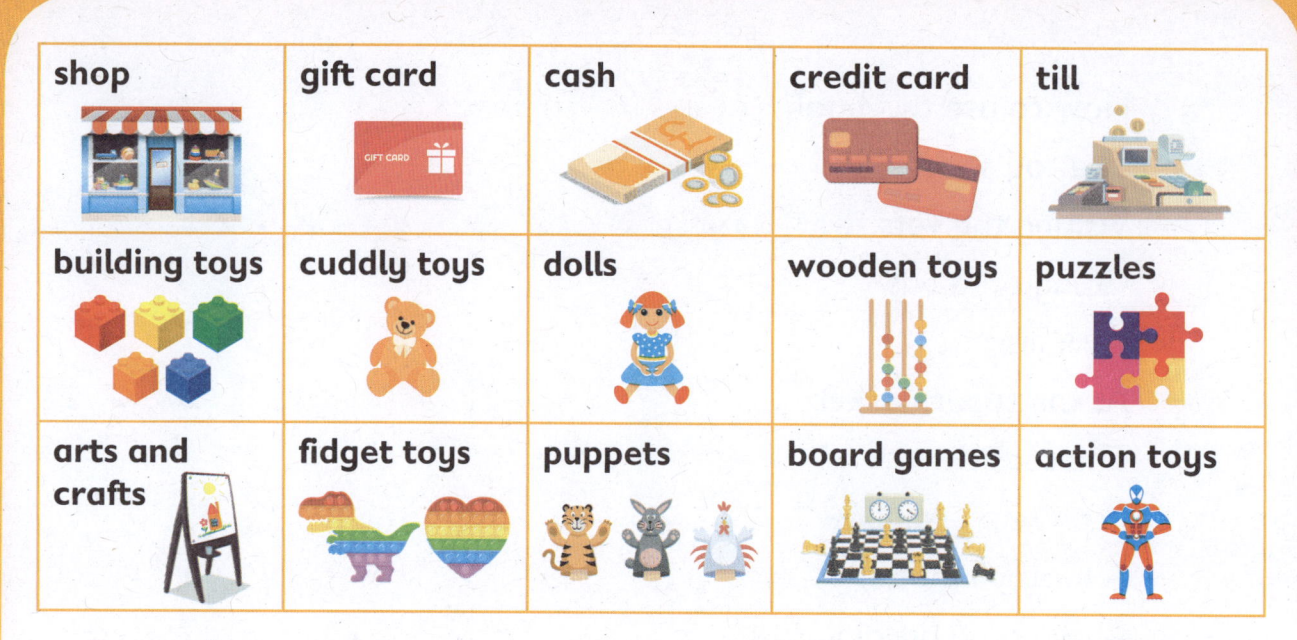

shop	gift card	cash	credit card	till
building toys	cuddly toys	dolls	wooden toys	puzzles
arts and crafts	fidget toys	puppets	board games	action toys

- Draw a line to match each picture to its partner. Now colour the pictures in.

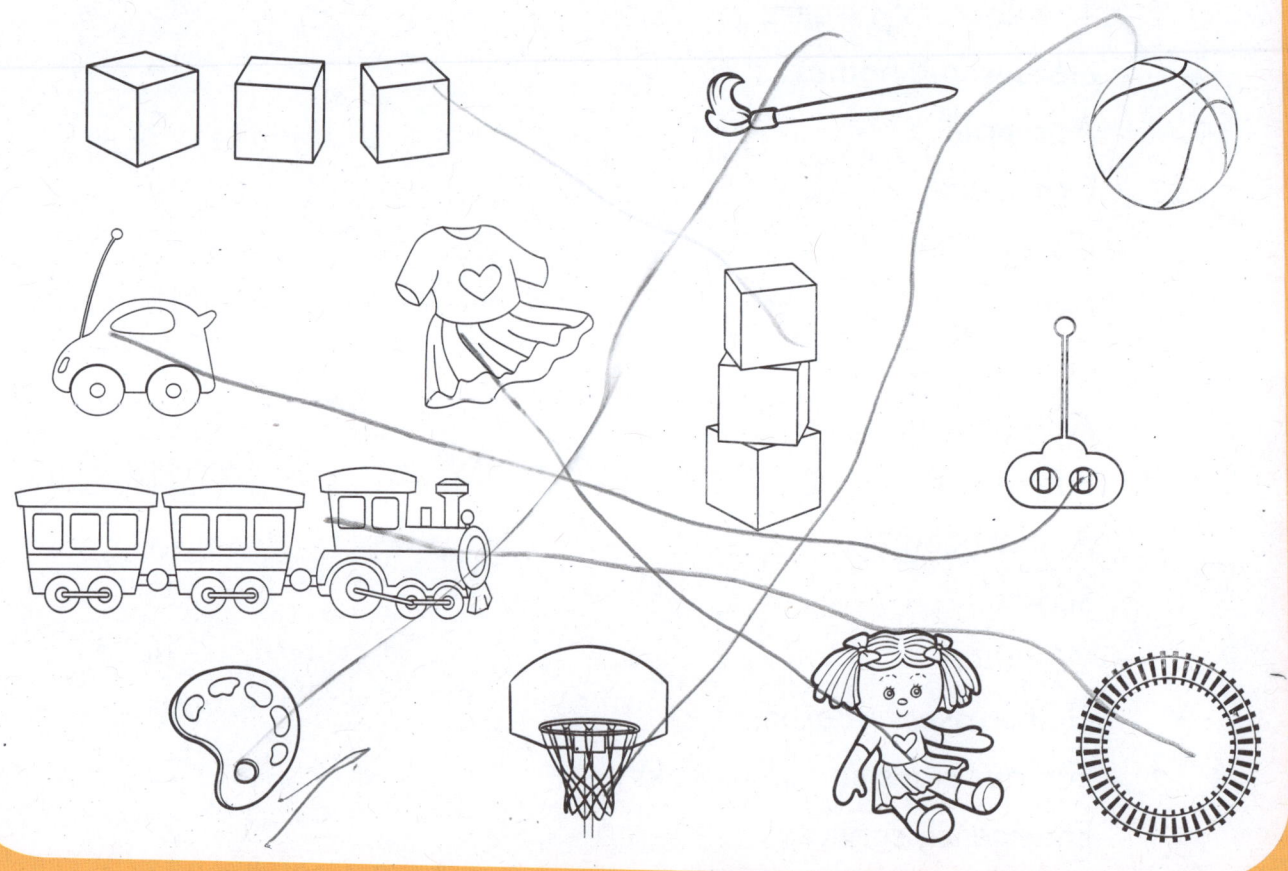

Encourage your child to talk about their experiences of visiting a toy shop. What would they like to buy and why? Tell them about your favourite toys as a child. Can they explain why their favourite toy is so special? When and where did they get it from? Does it have a name? Use words to describe time such as 'a long time ago', 'yesterday', 'when I was younger', 'recently'.

Try to make a kite and fly it together on a windy day.

Visiting the vets

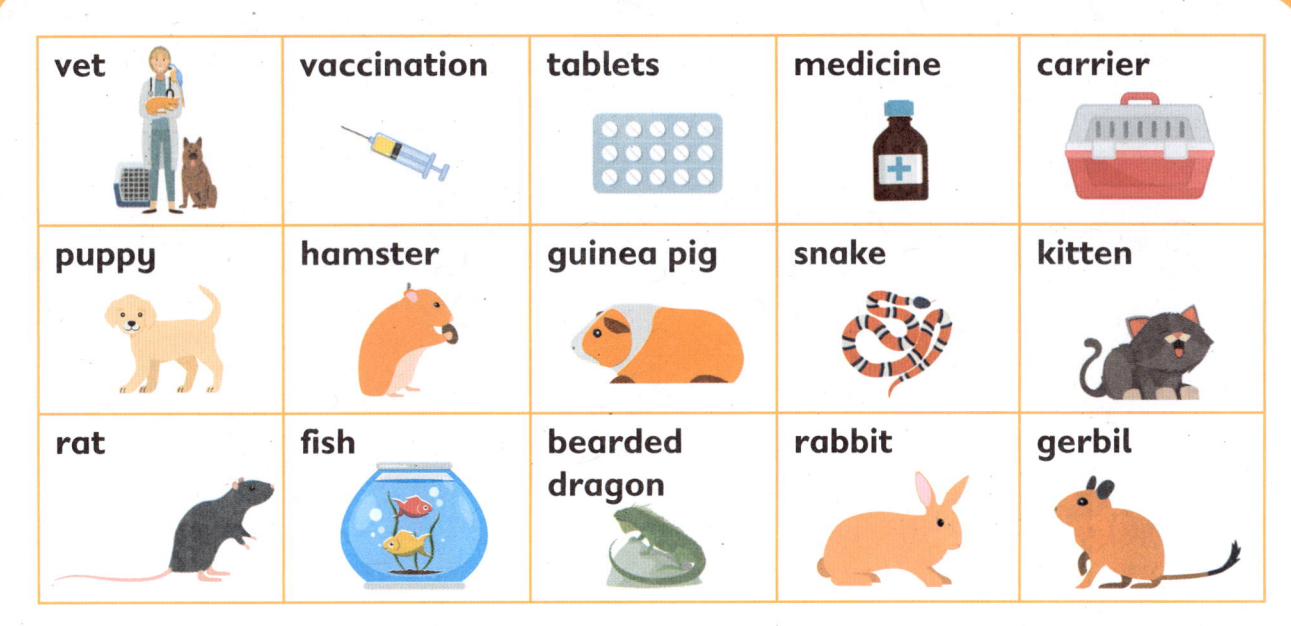

vet	vaccination	tablets	medicine	carrier
puppy	hamster	guinea pig	snake	kitten
rat	fish	bearded dragon	rabbit	gerbil

- Label the people, pets and items below using the pictures to help you.

vet tablets carrier

pupy hamster kitten

fish rabbit snake

- Do you have a pet? Would you like a pet? Draw a picture in the box below. You may like to name it too.

Going on a bus

bus	bus stop	journey	top deck	step
signal	bus pass	bell	seat	timetable
enter	exit	passenger	driver	inspector

- Write a label for each item and person that you see in the picture. Use the words above to help you.

Talk about… Have you ever been on a bus journey together? Where did you go? What did you see? How long did it take? How did you pay? Did you look at a timetable to see when the bus was due? Do all buses have two decks? Are all buses red? What do we call buses that go on long journeys? (coaches) Next time you go on a bus journey, play 'I spy' with your child, or count the blue cars. Make journeys fun.

Can your child make a bus model using reclaimable materials? What could they use for the bus, the wheels? Challenge them to get the wheels to turn around.

Park life

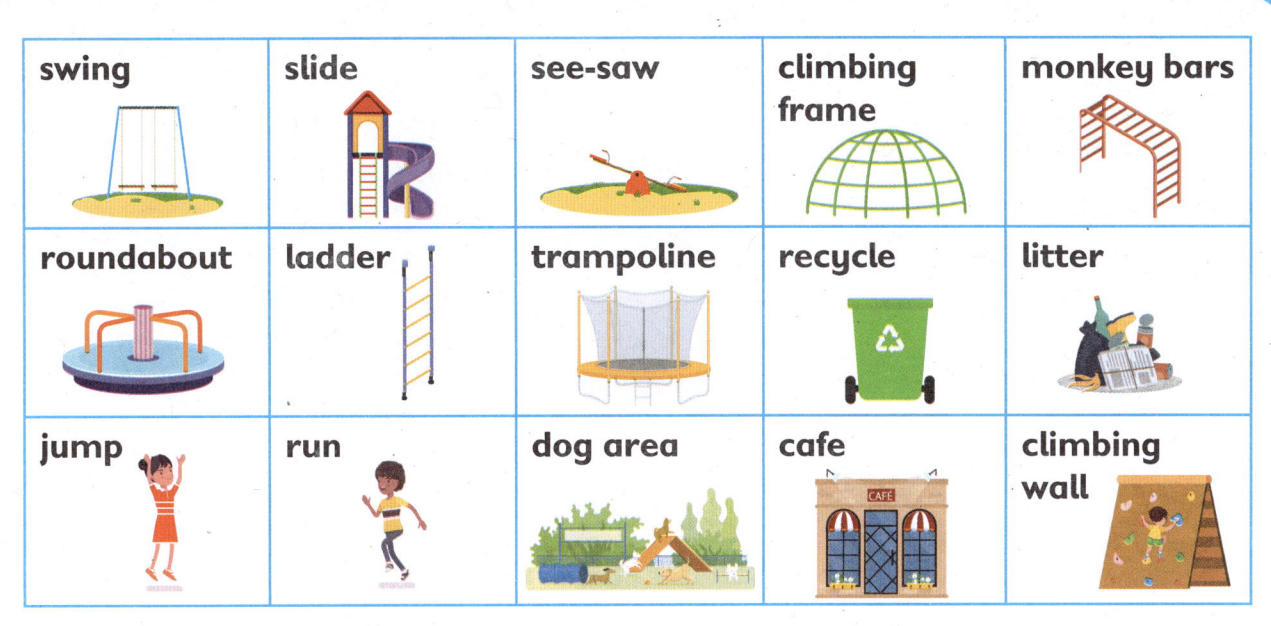

swing	slide	see-saw	climbing frame	monkey bars
roundabout	ladder	trampoline	recycle	litter
jump	run	dog area	cafe	climbing wall

- Draw a picture of you on your favourite piece of equipment.

- Complete the following sentences.

I am on _____.

I like it because _____.

You swing on the _____.

You spin on the _____.

You slide down the _____.

At the supermarket

shop	trolley	till	cashier	self-care
basket	conveyor belt	ready meals	bakery	dairy
fresh	fish counter	pet care	snacks	aisle

- Find the items on your shopping list on the supermarket shelves and tick them off.

My Shopping List
- bananas ☐
- dog food ☐
- popcorn ☐
- cheese ☐
- milk ☐
- apples ☐
- shampoo ☐
- ice lollies ☐
- chicken ☐
- bread ☐

Talk about a trip to the supermarket. What did you buy? Did you make a list? What else can be bought in a supermarket? How did you get there? How did you pay?

Write a shopping list together and use it on a shopping trip.

The seaside

sea	sand	beach	sandcastle	bucket
spade	ice cream	deckchair	hire	parasol
beach bat	crab	rock pool	beach ball	waves

- Draw a line to match each picture to its partner.

- What is your favourite flavour of ice cream? Why? Draw it in the box below.

I can see a rainbow

rainbow	red	orange	yellow	colours
blue	green	indigo	violet	sky
arc	seven	sunny	rain	pot of gold

- Fill in the blanks with words from the table above.

A rainbow is an arc made up of _____ colours.

The first colour is _____.

The last colour is _____.

A rainbow appears in the _____ when it is raining and _____ at the same time.

When the colours are seen together, they form an _____ shape.

Some people believe that there is a _____ ___ _____ at the end of the rainbow.

Teach your child this mnemonic to help them to remember the colours of the rainbow: **R**ichard **o**f **Y**ork **g**ave **b**attle **in** **v**ain. Talk about how rainbows are often seen as signs of hope and peace. Relate to the NHS rainbows seen during the Covid-19 pandemic. The rainbow represents freedom and diversity. It can be a symbol of hope during difficult times.

Blow some bubbles with your child. Can they spot any of the rainbow colours within the bubbles?

A football match

football	match	goal	game	flag
team	kit	pitch	stadium	ticket
whistle	referee	crowd	trophy	gate

- How many items can you see? Write the number at the bottom.

I can spy…

_____ goals _____ kits _____ whistles _____ tickets

_____ flag _____ footballs _____ trophies

- My favourite football team is _____.

A day on a building site

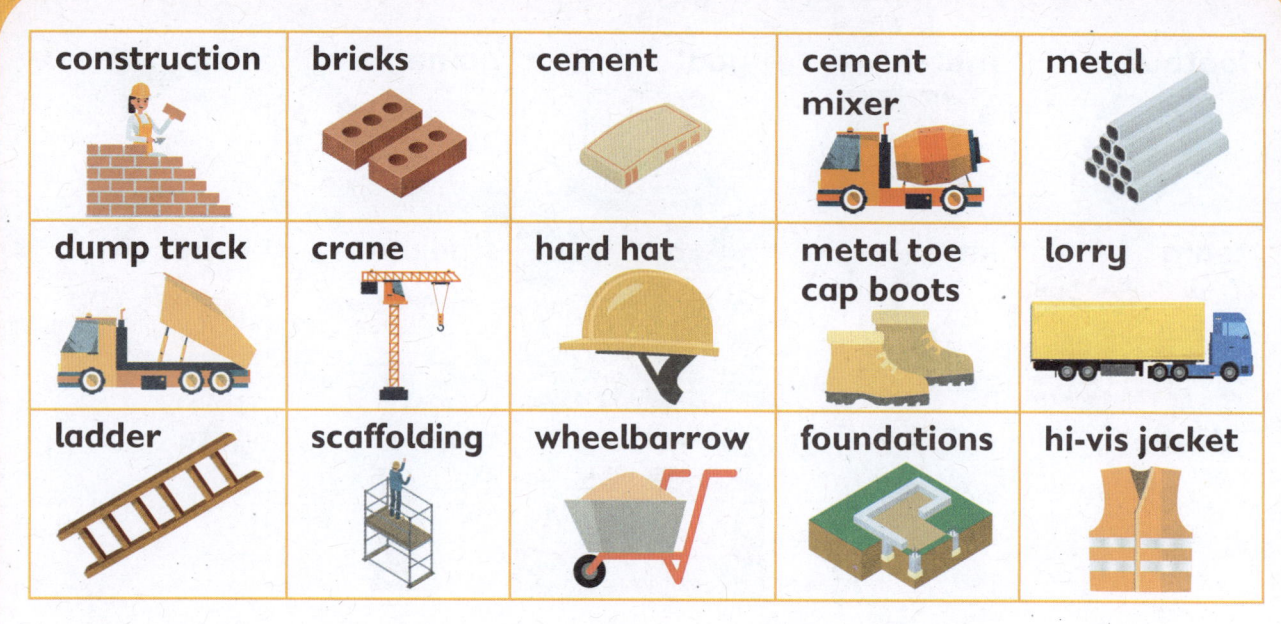

construction	bricks	cement	cement mixer	metal
dump truck	crane	hard hat	metal toe cap boots	lorry
ladder	scaffolding	wheelbarrow	foundations	hi-vis jacket

- Complete the sentences using the words and pictures above to help you.

Builders wear a _____ _____ to protect their heads.

Concrete is made in a _____ _____.

A wall is constructed using _____.

To climb up high you need a _____.

A _____ _____ transports the materials.

To keep safe on site you need to wear a _____ _____.

The first part of a building is called the _____.

- Circle the odd one out in each line.

metal toe cap boots	hard hat	hi-vis jacket	tie
cement	cement mixer	car	bricks
ladder	scaffolding	ice cream	crane

Talk to your child about the vocabulary. Is any of it new? Have they seen a building being constructed? Do they know what the foundations are? Why are these needed? Why is it important to keep safe on a building site? How do people do this?

Look at famous buildings from around the world together.

The doctors' surgery

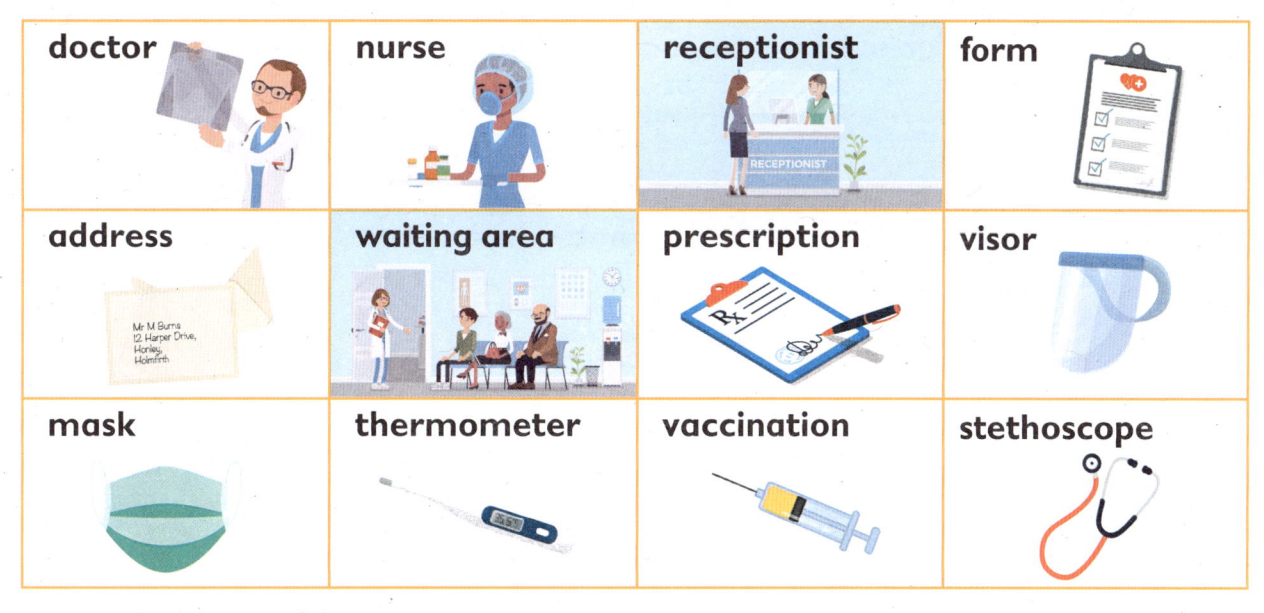

doctor	nurse	receptionist	form
address	waiting area	prescription	visor
mask	thermometer	vaccination	stethoscope

- Draw a line to match each word to its picture.

nurse   doctor   stethoscope   visor   prescription   thermometer   form

- Are there any words which you didn't know before? Write them down and draw pictures to help you remember them.

Houses and homes

house	detached	terraced	semi-detached	igloo
mud hut	bungalow	houseboat	mansion	teepee
caravan	farmhouse	cottage	log cabin	yurt

- Label each house or home picture that you see using the names from above. Now colour in each home.

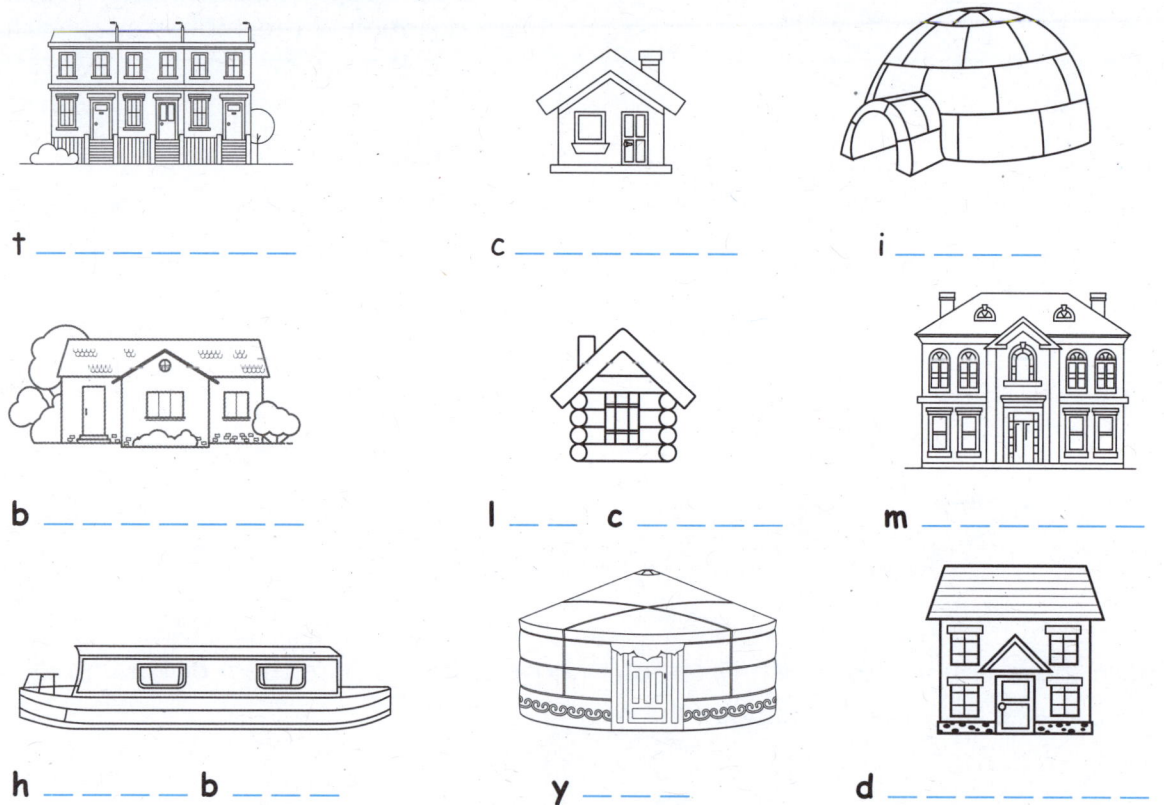

t _ _ _ _ _ _ _ _

c _ _ _ _ _ _ _

i _ _ _ _ _

b _ _ _ _ _ _ _ _

l _ _   c _ _ _ _

m _ _ _ _ _ _ _

h _ _ _ _ b _ _ _ _

y _ _ _

d _ _ _ _ _ _ _ _

Talk to your child about the new vocabulary. Is any of it new? Do they know where in the world you may see a yurt, igloo, houseboat? Talk about your home. What type of home is it? What do 'detached' and 'terraced' mean?

Walk around your local area and look at the types of houses and homes. Talk about the names of them.

At school

school	classroom	playground	dining hall
entrance	play time	lunchtime	teacher
assembly	corridor	staff room	medical room

- Draw a plan of your school in the box below. Include all the items in the list.

    1. Teacher
    2. Classroom
    3. Playground
    4. Staff room
    5. Dining hall (or where you eat lunch)
    6. Medical room
    7. Entrance

Into space

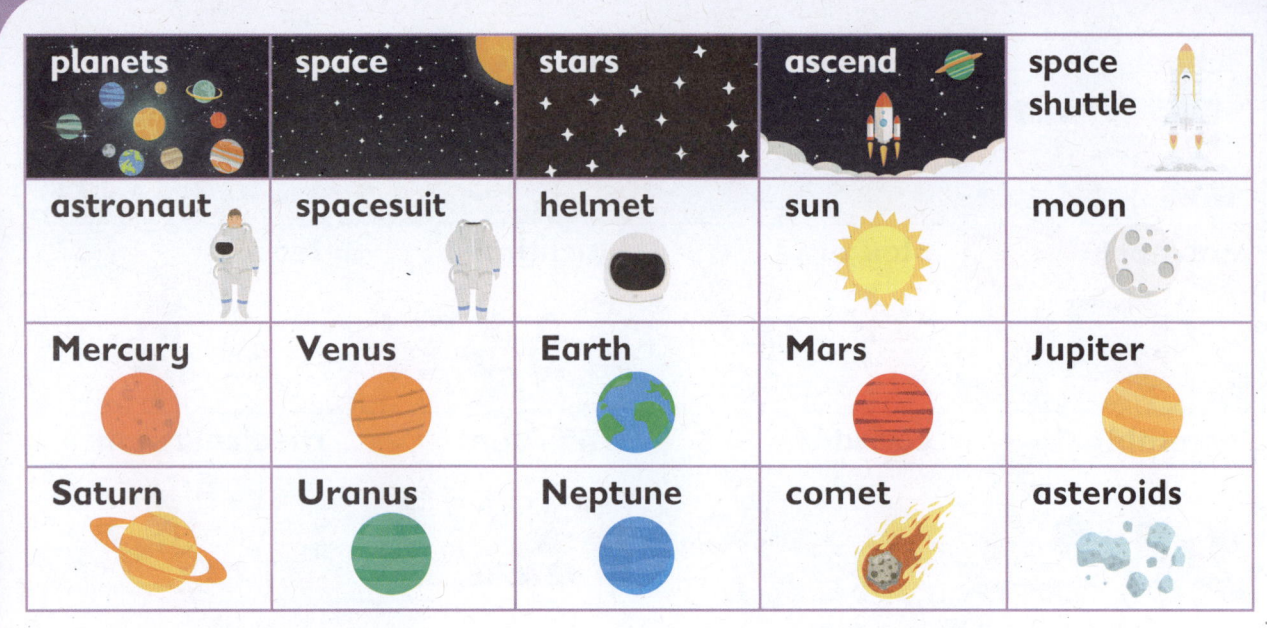

planets	space	stars	ascend	space shuttle
astronaut	spacesuit	helmet	sun	moon
Mercury	Venus	Earth	Mars	Jupiter
Saturn	Uranus	Neptune	comet	asteroids

- Look at the pictures below. Write a sentence about each picture.

Encourage your child to name and order the planets. Try this mnemonic: '**M**any **v**ery **e**lderly **m**en **j**ust **s**nooze **u**nder **n**ewspapers'. Show them photographs of the planets and talk about the differences in appearance. Which planet do we live on? What is our planet like? What do they think about life on other planets?

Use various sized balls to create your own solar system. If balls are not available, you could cut and stick paper planets. Make a display and regularly visit until your child knows the names and the order.

Can you fix it?

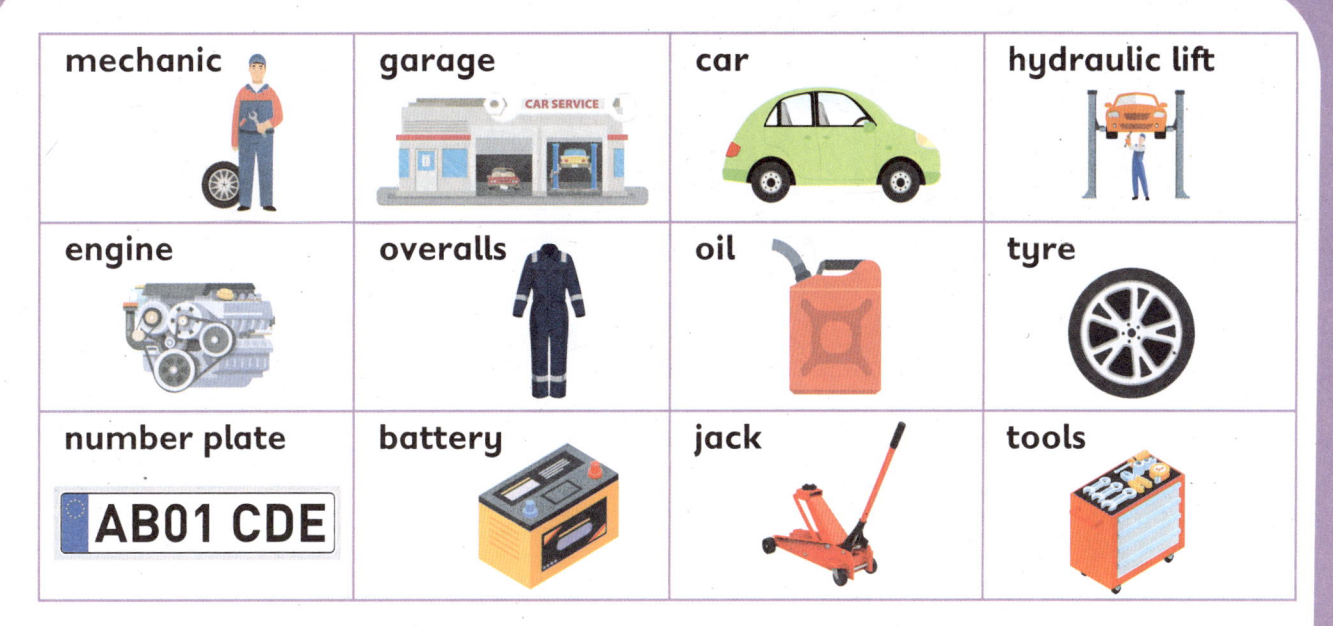

mechanic	garage	car	hydraulic lift
engine	overalls	oil	tyre
number plate AB01 CDE	battery	jack	tools

- Look at following picture. Circle all the items and people listed above that you can see.

- Now write about what you spotted on the lines below. Use the words in the box.

| mechanic | fix | tools | engine | car |

_____
_____
_____

Nocturnal creatures

night-time	daytime	nocturnal	diurnal	eyesight
caves	toad	bat	fox	hedgehog
badger	owl	mouse	hamster	hunting

- Are these animals diurnal or nocturnal? Draw lines to match them to the correct picture.

Diurnal (active in the daytime)

Nocturnal (active at night-time)

Talk to your child about 'nocturnal' and what it means. Explain that some animals have had to adapt to be able to survive in the dark, for example owls have huge eyes. Has your child ever seen any nocturnal animals in the daytime? Find out more about being a nocturnal creature.

Create daytime and night-time pictures using crayons or paints. Compare them using some of the new vocabulary they have learnt.

Fruit smoothie fun

wash hands	peel	cut	half	quarter
seeds	pips	strawberries	melon	grapes
kiwi	raspberries	blueberries	pineapple	mango

- Draw pictures of all the fruit you would choose to make your favourite smoothie. Write their names too.

- Write **true** or **false** next to these sentences.

    A strawberry is a fruit that makes a good smoothie. _____

    Before you make a smoothie, you need to chop the fruit. _____

    A cuddly toy would taste nice in a smoothie. _____

    Mangoes need to be peeled before using them in a smoothie. _____

    Combine means to put all the ingredients together. _____

    You do not need to wash your hands before making a smoothie. _____

    Eating a smoothie with a knife and fork is best. _____

At the farm

owl	owlet	goat	kid	combine harvester
frog	froglet	pastoral	arable	tractor
horse	foal	goose	gosling	quad bike

- Draw a line to match each picture to its partner.

- Complete these sentences using the words in the box.

| arable | pastoral | combine harvester |

A _____ farm keeps animals.

Crops and vegetables are grown on an _____ farm.

A _____ is a machine used to help farmers to gather crops.

Ask your child to explain the two types of farms to you. Do they know the names of baby animals? Can they think of any other animals and babies, such as cow and calf?

Use a paper plate or circle of paper to create a sheep or lamb. Add cotton wool or wool to make it realistic. Think about the colour of the sheep's eyes and ears.

Eating out

table	waitress	waiter	service
menu	starter	main	dessert
napkin	tip	tray	bill

- Copy five words from above. Draw pictures to help you to remember their meaning.

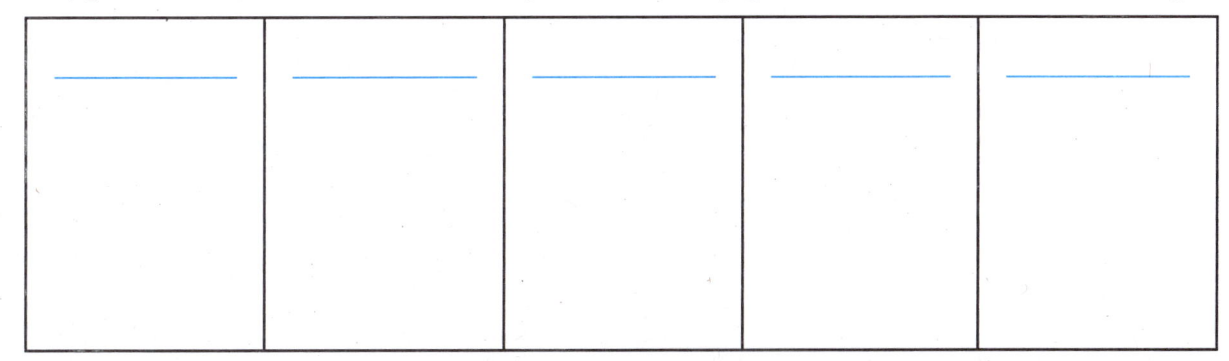

- What is your favourite meal to eat? Draw it on the plate.

My favourite meal is _____.

- Do you know how to ask for the bill in a restaurant in another language?

　🇫🇷　L'addition, s'il vous plaît.　　🇪🇸　La cuenta, por favor.

　🇩🇪　Die Rechnung, bitte!　　🇮🇹　Il conto, per favore.

21

A new baby

newborn baby	sibling	bottle	milk	scratch mittens
nappy	hat	buggy	cot	rattle
changing mat	Baby-gro	hospital bracelet	Moses basket	blanket

- Write a list of all the things that a newborn baby may need. Use the words above. You may also have some ideas of your own.

  1. _____
  2. _____
  3. _____
  4. _____
  5. _____

- Answer the clues using the words in the table.

  A baby may sleep in this…   _____

  This toy makes a noise…   _____

  A baby may drink milk from this…   _____

  Instead of using a toilet, a baby has a… _____

Having a new baby sibling can be exciting but also worrying for some children. They may worry about how things will change in your family. Encourage them to help you prepare for a new baby. Talk about what a baby will need and why. Read stories about new babies.

Ask your child to design a Baby-gro for a baby. What pattern might they put on the Baby-gro?

Sports

tennis	football	rugby	swimming
athletics	gymnastics	hockey	trampolining
cycling	skiing	badminton	volleyball

- Look at the pictures below and label the sports.

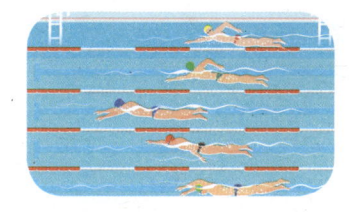

- Rewrite these sentences so that they make sense.

gymnast flips Sophie the bar. on over the

_____

a footballer goal. The scored Alex

_____

shaped. rugby is oval A ball

_____

high can on a trampoline. You bounce

_____

23

Weather

sun	rain	fog	snow	floods
thunder and lightning	climate	sleet	wind	tsunami
monsoon	hail	temperature	mist	hurricane

- Look at the pictures and words below. Circle the correct word for each picture.

sleet / hail / sun

thunder and lightning / snow / flood

monsoon / rain / fog

floods / mist / hurricane

fog / sun / hail

monsoon / snow / mist

Weather can evoke excitement in children, especially extreme types of weather. Ask your child which weather types they already know. Talk about weather in different countries. Ask them to explain the meaning of any new words. What is their favourite type of weather and why? You may like to talk about suitable clothes for different weather.

Create a mobile of different weather types using a coat hanger.

24

Hairdressers / Barbers

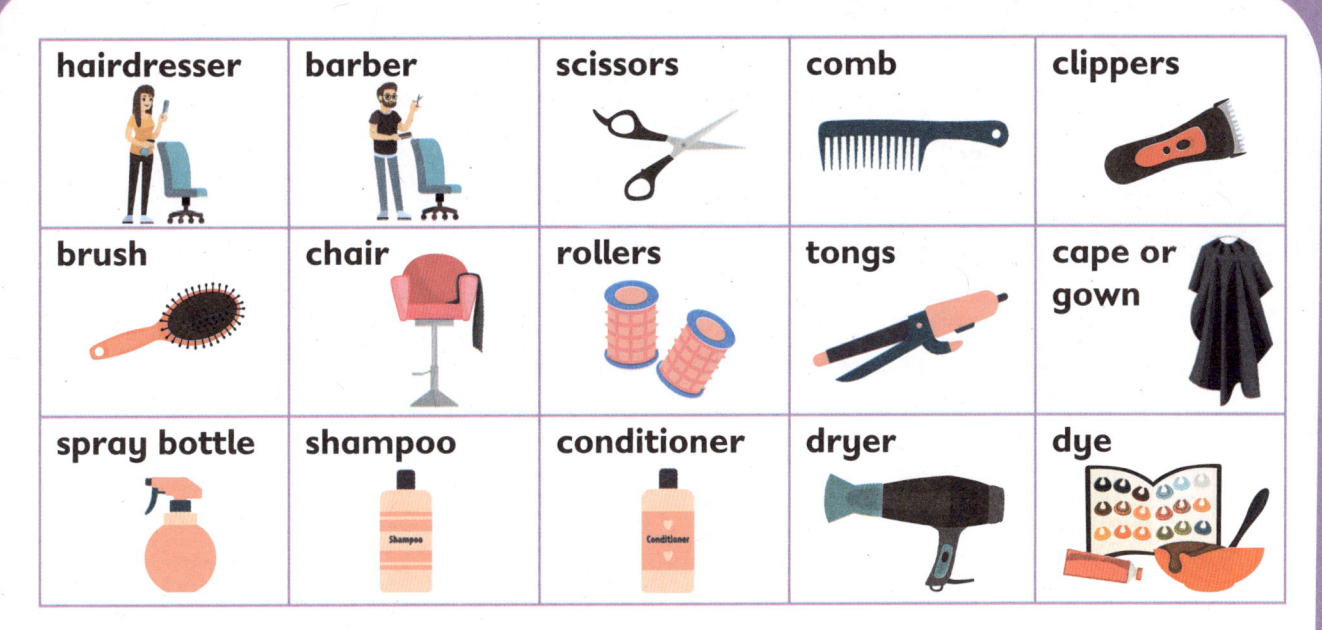

hairdresser	barber	scissors	comb	clippers
brush	chair	rollers	tongs	cape or gown
spray bottle	shampoo	conditioner	dryer	dye

- Look at the picture. Circle all the items and people listed above that you can see.

- Draw a picture of you with a new haircut. You may like to choose a different colour or shape. How do you look?

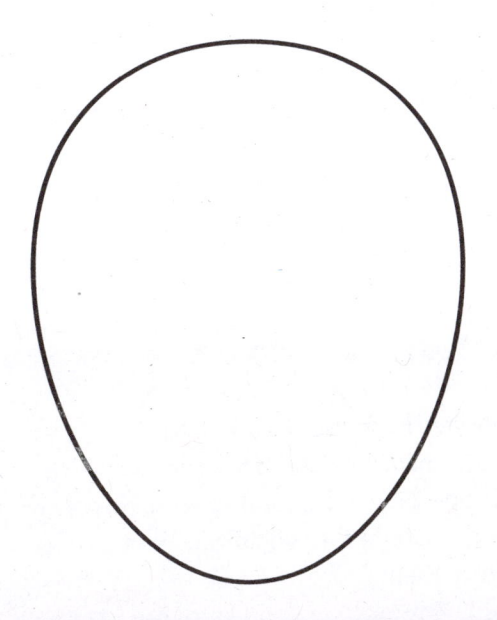

Famous cities and landmarks

Country	Landmark	City
United Kingdom	Big Ben	London
France	Eiffel Tower	Paris
Italy	Colosseum	Rome
Spain	Sagrada Família	Barcelona
USA	Statue of Liberty	New York
Australia	Opera House	Sydney

- Draw a line to match each landmark to its city.

London   Sydney   New York   Paris   Barcelona   Rome

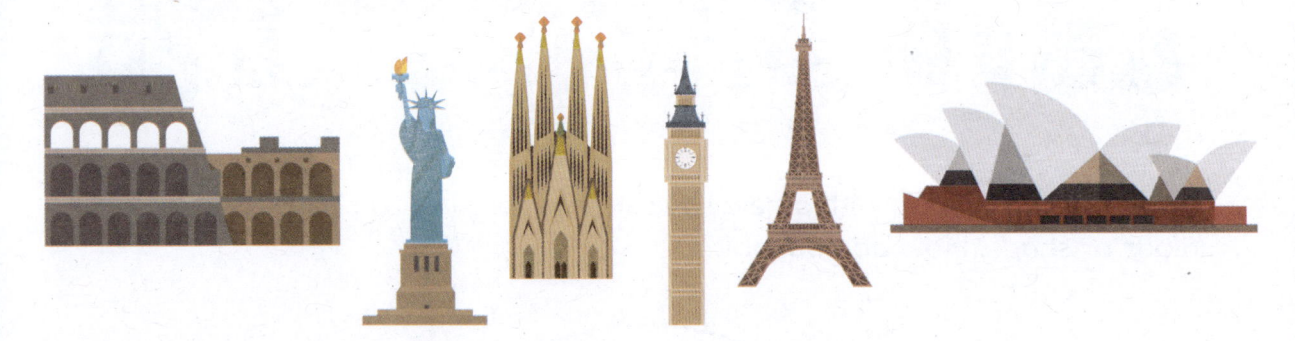

- Complete the sentences below.

   My favourite landmark is _____

   I like it best because _____

Talk to your child about the landmarks. Have they visited any of them? Have you? Look at similarities and differences between them. Ask them which one they like best and why. Do they know where the countries are in the world? Look at a map or globe together to locate them.

Make a 3D model of your child's favourite landmark. You could use building blocks or reclaimed materials.

Emergency services

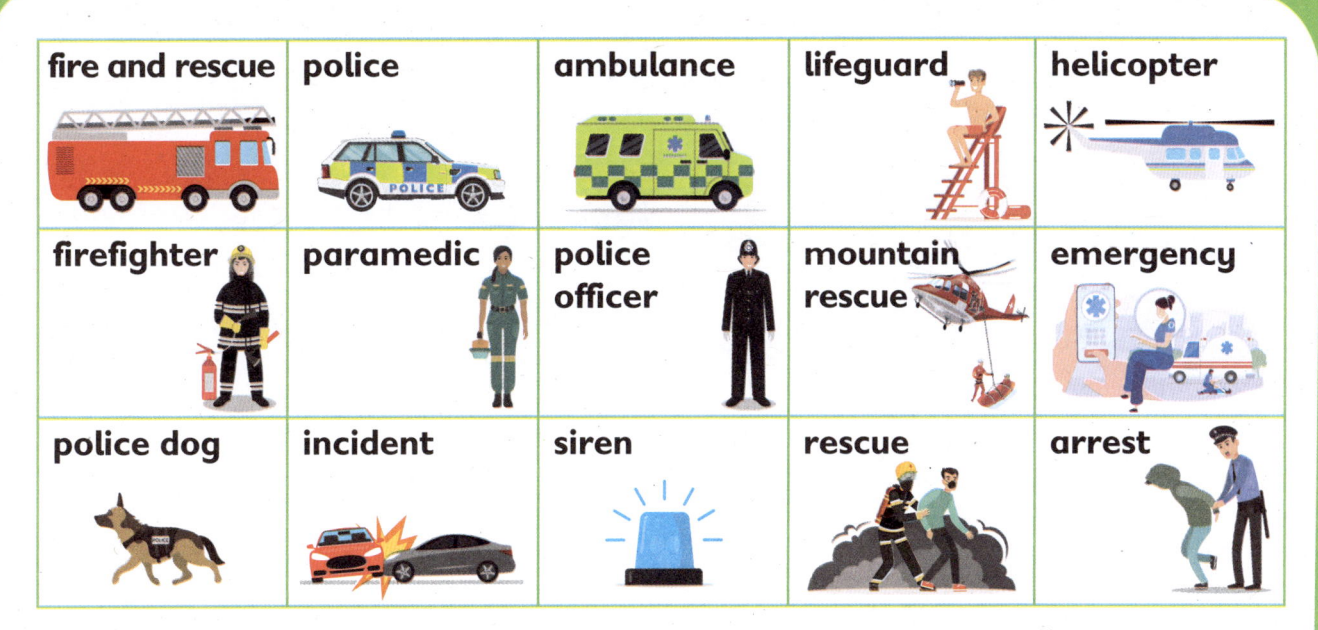

fire and rescue	police	ambulance	lifeguard	helicopter
firefighter	paramedic	police officer	mountain rescue	emergency
police dog	incident	siren	rescue	arrest

- Find 13 vocabulary words in the grid below. Tick them off as you find them.

a	m	b	u	l	a	n	c	e	q	m	n	x	f	y	p	q
r	o	y	g	i	p	a	r	a	m	e	d	i	c	h	o	a
r	f	v	a	f	i	r	e	f	i	g	h	t	e	r	l	e
e	f	l	i	e	m	e	r	g	e	n	c	y	q	s	i	h
s	i	p	a	g	e	t	g	y	a	u	v	k	o	i	c	q
t	c	c	d	u	h	g	t	j	o	e	z	s	b	r	e	e
l	e	h	c	a	z	h	g	q	c	h	o	s	o	e	z	u
h	r	s	v	r	i	b	v	i	n	c	i	d	e	n	t	c
a	e	y	z	d	s	i	l	z	h	j	a	l	a	h	o	s
r	b	h	d	e	d	o	g	m	s	b	d	z	a	o	t	e
o	m	i	p	e	p	s	h	e	l	i	c	o	p	t	e	r

- Complete the sentences below.

You will need to call the _____ to help this man.

You will need to call the _____ if this is happening.

My favourite rescue service is _____.

Recycling

recycle	reuse	environment	glass
paper / card	cans	fabric	compost
electronics	batteries	plastic	upcycle

- Draw lines to match the type of recycling to the correct bin. The first one is done for you.

  PLASTIC   GLASS   CANS   CARD   COMPOST

- Complete these sentences using the words in the box.

  | recycle | environment | garden | compost | trousers | fabric |

  I can _____ my old _____ in the _____ recycle bin.

  It is important to recycle to protect our _____.

  The _____ waste can be made into _____.

Does your child help with the recycling? Can they tell you which bin the items should go into? Talk about why recycling is important for protecting and prolonging our world.

Have a go at making some paper with your child. Soak scraps of paper in hot soapy water for about 30 minutes, then mix until they make a paste. Squeeze all the water out and lay flat on a tea towel, then roll it out flat between two tea towels. You may like to iron the mixture. Leave for 24 hours to dry. It's ready to use.

Flying high

airport	security	check in	cabin crew	travelator
duty free	pilot	control tower	passport	passenger
luggage	boarding pass	boarding gate	runway	waiting area

- Look at the picture. Circle all the items and people listed above that you can see.

- Think about what you would need to take on your holiday. Draw all the items you need inside the suitcase below. Label them if you can.

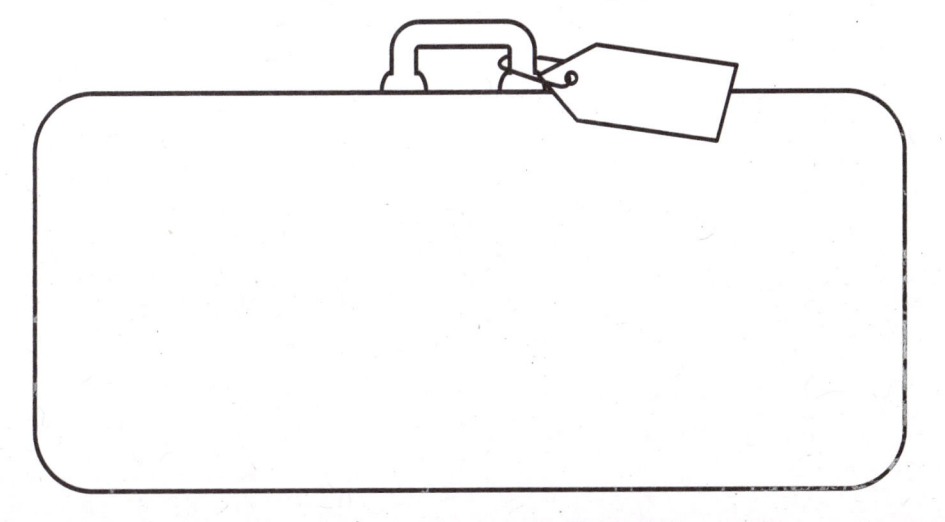

29

Train journey

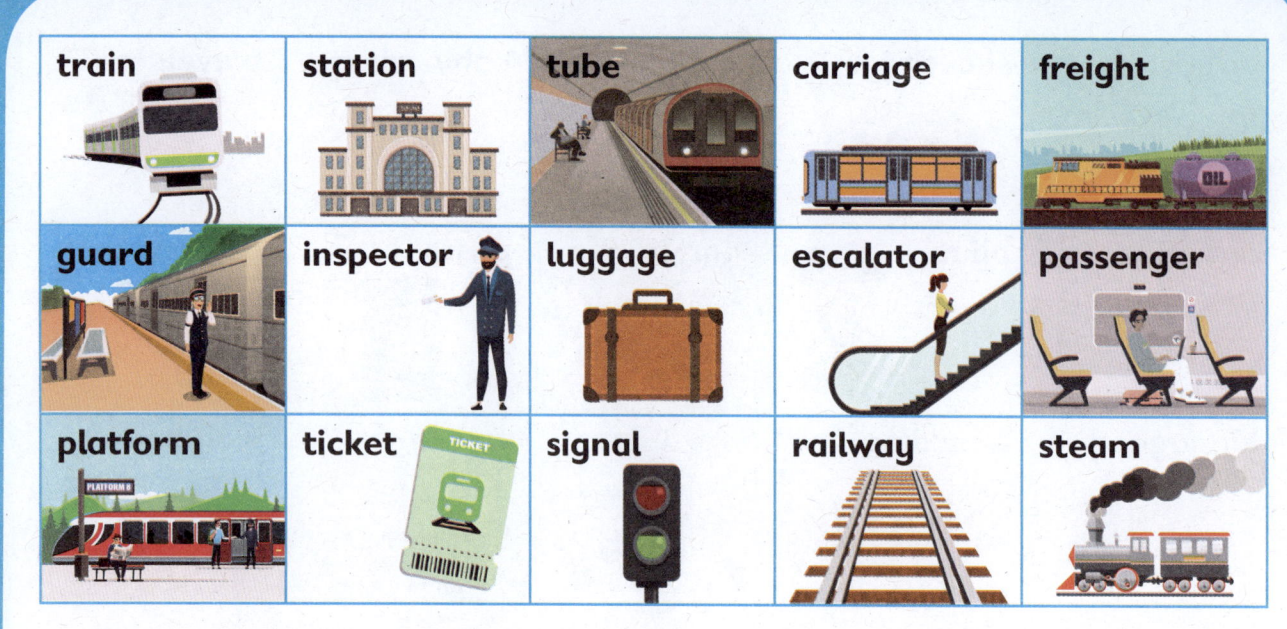

train	station	tube	carriage	freight
guard	inspector	luggage	escalator	passenger
platform	ticket	signal	railway	steam

- Draw a picture to match each statement.

This person checks tickets on a train.	You wait for a train on this.
You take this on the train with your belongings in.	This is a fast underground train.

Help your child to find all the words from the vocabulary box above, then use the leftover letters to reveal a secret message.

c	o	t	r	a	i	n	n	g	r	l	i	p
a	p	l	a	t	f	o	r	m	t	a	n	a
f	r	e	i	g	h	t	u	l	a	n	s	s
t	i	o	l	u	g	g	a	g	e	g	p	s
n	m	s	w	y	o	u	h	a	t	i	e	e
v	a	c	a	r	r	i	a	g	e	s	c	n
e	e	f	y	i	n	i	s	u	k	h	t	g
e	t	u	b	e	d	t	h	a	c	e	o	e
e	s	c	a	l	a	t	o	r	i	b	r	r
s	t	a	t	i	o	n	o	d	t	o	k	!

30

KS1 common exception words

Tick the word once if you can **READ** it, twice if you can **SPELL** it and three times if you can **WRITE** it. Use the blank spaces to write your favourite new words from this book to practise them.

Word	R	S	W	Word	R	S	W	Word	R	S	W
the				you				I			
a				your				there			
do				they				today			
to				be							
of				me							
said				she							
says				we							
are				no							
were				go							
was				so							
is				by							
his				my							
has				here							

Answers

Page 4
- Child to colour the pictures in.

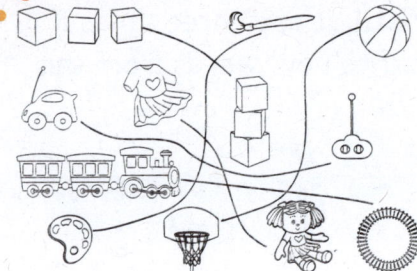

Page 5
- vet; tablets; carrier
  puppy; hamster; kitten
  fish; rabbit; snake
- Child to draw a picture of a pet.

Page 6
- Child to write labels for bus, bus stop, top deck, seat, passenger, driver and inspector.

Page 7
- Child to draw a picture of themselves on their favourite piece of park equipment.
- Child to complete the sentences.

Page 8
- Child to find the items on the shopping list in the supermarket picture and tick them off.

Page 9
- Child to draw a picture of their favourite ice cream.

Page 10
- seven; red; violet; sky; sunny; arc; pot of gold

Page 11
- 10 goals; 8 kits; 9 whistles; 6 tickets; 6 flags; 7 footballs; 12 trophies
- Child to write down the name of their favourite football team.

Page 12
- hard hat; cement mixer; bricks; ladder; dump truck; hi-vis jacket; foundations
- tie; car; ice cream

Page 13
- Child to write down words they didn't know before and draw pictures.

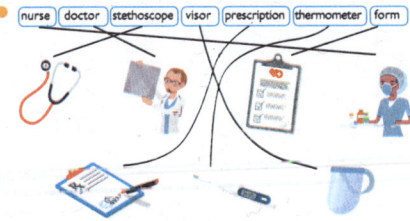

Page 14
- terraced; cottage; igloo
  bungalow; log cabin; mansion
  houseboat; yurt; detached
- Child to colour pictures in.

Page 15
- Child to draw a plan of their school including the items in the list.

Page 16
- Child to write their own sentences about each picture. Examples:
  The space shuttle ascends into space.
  The space shuttle launches.
  There are two planets in the sky.
  The astronaut is floating in space.
  I can see the moon and stars in the sky.
  A comet flies through the sky.

Page 17
- Child to write about what the spotted in the picture. Example:
  The mechanic uses tools to fix the car engine.

Page 18

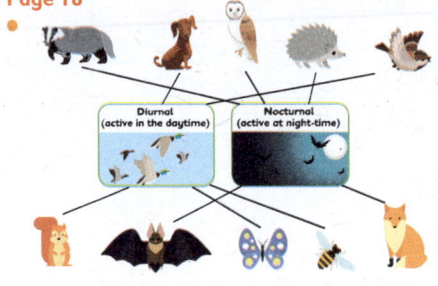

Page 19
- Child to draw pictures of fruit in the smoothie maker. Child to write the names of the fruit.
- true; true; false; true; true; false; false

Page 20
- pastoral; arable; combine harvester

Page 21
- Child to copy words and draw pictures.
- Child to draw favourite meal on the plate. Child to write down what their favourite meal is.

Page 22
- Child to write a list of things that you need for a newborn baby.
- cot; rattle; bottle; nappy

Page 23
- tennis; badminton; skiing
  swimming; volleyball; cycling
- Sophie the gymnast flips over on the bar.
  The footballer Alex scored a goal.
  A rugby ball is oval shaped.
  You can bounce high on a trampoline.

Page 24
- sleet; thunder and lightning
  fog; hurricane
  hail; snow

Page 25
- Child to draw a picture of their new haircut.

Page 26
- Child to complete the sentences.

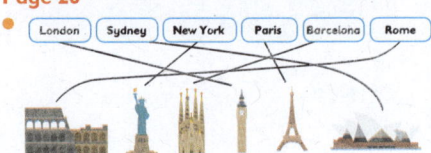

Page 27
- Child to complete the sentences.

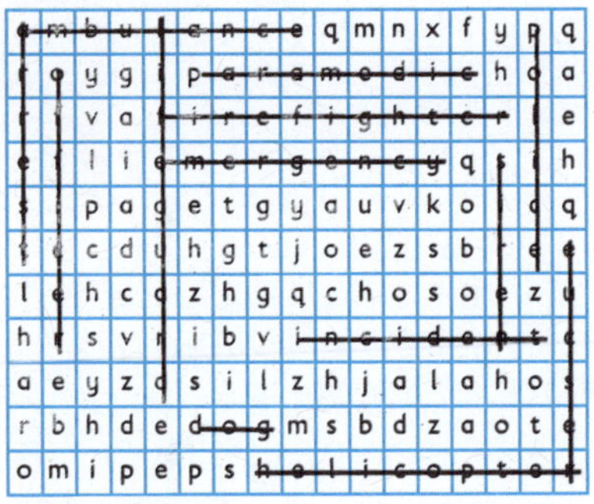

Page 28
- recycle, trousers, fabric
  environment
  garden, compost

Page 29
- Child to draw items they would take on holiday and label if possible.

Page 30
- Child to draw a picture for each statement. 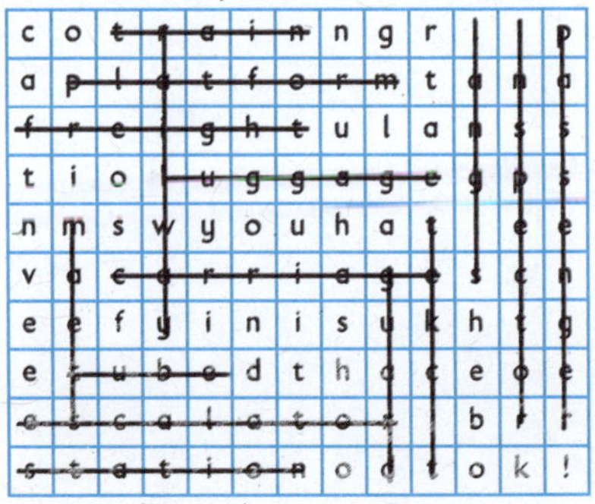
- Secret message: congratulations you have finished the book!